© 2022.

Yanique Renwick
The Black Trojan Woman
All rights reserved. No part of this publication may be reproduced, stored in a retrieval system or transmited in any form or by any means, electronic, mechanical, photocopying, recording or otherwise without the prior permision of the publisher or in accordance with the provisions of the Copyright, Designs and Patents Act 1988 or under the terms of any licence permitting limited copying issued by the Copyright Licensing Angency.

Published by: Yanique Renwick

Illustrated by: Gabriel Montalvo

Cover Design by: Gabriel Montalvo

A CIP record for this book is acailable from the Library of Congress Cataloging-in-Publication Data

ISBN: 978-0-578-38510-5

Publisher Number For Title Management: 2071074

ABOUT THE AUTHOR

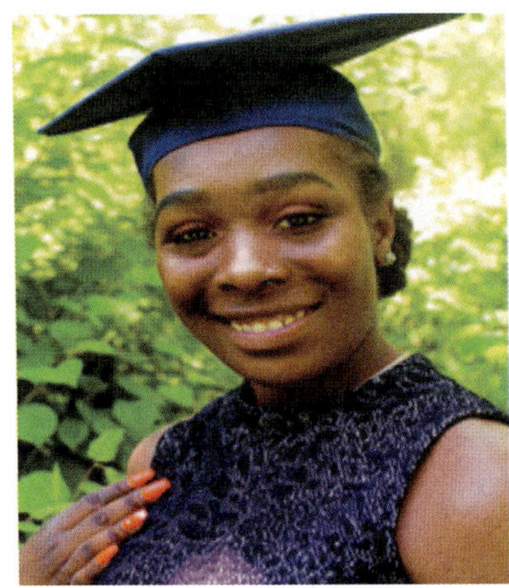

Yanique Renwick is a graduate of Lincoln University, PA with a Bachelor's in Human Services. She chose this degree path because of the burning desire to help others that has been instilled since birth. This book is meant to serve as inspirational work. The purpose of her writing is to show others that that life eventually works itself out. Believing we experience trauma to build our mental and emotional endurance; we should look for the lesson in everything we experience. The author hopes you gain life lessons through the poetry and stories told throughout this book.

Prologue:

I am writing this entire book with one hand.

Continue reading to find out why

Plase enjoy!

THE BLACK TROJAN WOMAN

YANIQUE RENWICK

PART I

As a child, I always had many friends; but only 1 best friend, Destiny. We met and became friends in kindergarten; a time when life was much simpler. The days of meeting one another and then 5 minutes later playing like we have known each other for years. We also went to the same dance school, so we became remarkably close. Dance is my first love; before any boy ever came in the picture, there was always dance. I never thought she'd leave me. I remember making music videos with my dad in the living room, rapping quite terribly, and musically moving to the rhythm of fifty cents' "candy shop". After school, I attended dance classes. I always had ballet first, then jazz, then tap. After tap was always African or hip hop. African dance was my favorite; it felt so freeing. I must have felt the connection to my ancestors before I even knew the connection existed. So, from childhood to adulthood, I have had a free spirit and one that needs to be expressed. I also played the piano and did a couple of plays in elementary school. There was one in particular where I had the role of a teacher. During practice, I would feel lightheaded and randomly get headaches. I would often ask to sit down, but the teacher, Ms. Bell, would get upset with me because she considered me taking frequent, unscheduled breaks as being lazy. When she said "no" to my request of sitting down, I would ask to go to the bathroom instead. During this brief period of alone time, I would sit on the toilet just to get a break and rest my head in my hands, massaging my temples. I tigued, and I brushed it off as low blood sugar. The constant fatigue was such a battle within me, having the energy of an 80-year-old but the spirit of a rambunctious 9-year-old. This caused some mind-body warfare, and in turn, I began to feel unhappy with myself. I had extreme headaches that felt like someone was pinching my brain and refused to let go, no matter how hard I tried to fight it. There were times this pain was so gruesome I would go to the long red couch, with a floral design against the back wall of the living room in my great grandfather's house, and just lay there in agony. Sometimes, I missed family gatherings because of how awful I felt. Unfortunately, I was not particularly good at communicating this, but my family would take care of me regardless. No one knew what was going on with me. I missed my fifth-grade graduation from P.S.136, and we only lived about fifty feet away from the school. Although soon after I would be moving to a better neighborhood in terms of schooling. Long Island is noticeably quiet, which is a peculiar feeling, coming from Queens and originally living on a busy street. Here, I had my own room, and my mother painted the walls my favorite color, purple. As a little girl, I was always full of life, without a care in the world. My parents were no longer together, and I was too young to ever remember them being in a relationship that was not strictly co-parenting. Since I have always lived with my mother, she had to see much more with me. I did however always have a relationship with my dad. I was a daddy's girl until around the age of 8. Eventually, I moved to Long Island, and he reminded me to stay true to my Queens roots.

January 2nd, 2009, is a day I will always remember.

I was nine years old when I had my first seizure. Earlier that day, I felt very fatigued and dizzy. My mother thought I was just being dramatic because I tended to hyperbolize at times. This was not one of those times. I was complaining about my fatigue and kept going to the living room couch to lay down to regain energy. She yelled "Yani, get up what are you doing! Just come eat something, you are being a drama queen, as usual!" I thought for a moment, maybe I was just being dramatic. So, I tried to shake it off and complied. I went to the kitchen to cut a piece of sweet potato pie that my great aunt gave us from Christmas dinner. I took out a small white plate from the above cabinet and a knife from the silverware drawer. As I began to cut the pie, I felt myself becoming dizzier as the seconds passed. I put the knife down and leaned on the counter in an attempt to collect myself, the plate was close to the edge. I abruptly fell to the kitchen floor, and so did the empty plate. I was having a seizure. I know when people hear the word seizure, they think of a person shaking uncontrollably, but I was stiff as aboard. I had more than one occurrence that day. During another episode, I stumbled backward towards the microwave cart, next to my room and I hit the back of my head on it (BOOM). To this day I can still feel a slight pain in that area when I think about it. Trauma is powerful. My mother was scared to death. I remember coming to a bit and hearing her run to the house phone to call 911. The person on the phone proceeded to give her life-saving directions. She asked me simple questions in urgency, such as, "What is your name?", she asked, "What year is it?" Her goal was to assess my mental state while trying to maintain my consciousness.

After she got me off the floor and onto my bed, we sat there together. Looking up to her with curiosity, I asked her, "How can you possibly be so calm?" She said, "I'm not, but if I'm freaking out and acting worried then you will too. I have to set an example."

She was right about this- because deep down I knew if I saw her innermost feeling on the outside, that would incite a feeling of fear in me. My mother had to be so extremely strong for me, and I forever commend her for that.

The ambulance waited outside of my house as I was rushed into the back of it. My mother nervously climbed aboard, not knowing where this journey would take us. I began to worry on the way there because of the uncertainty of what was going to happen or what was wrong. I recalled having severe headaches for months prior, so I knew it related to that, and the obvious convulsions I experienced. The ride to the hospital was surprisingly fast. When we arrived, I was rolled into the emergency room on the gurney and the doctors and nurses began performing tests on me, which seemed like it was never-ending. I spent days in the ER but eventually, the doctors transferred me to the Pediatric Intensive Care Unit (ICU). Which I was not excited about because then I knew there was something seriously wrong, but when I heard there was a playroom and this was a section of the hospital just for kids, I got excited. I only had to share the room with one other girl, as opposed to the ER with everyone who comes in for everything from a head injury to a broken toe. They continued to perform tests, probing, and prodding to figure out what exactly was wrong. I remember doctors and nurses coming in and asking my mother the same kinds of questions repeatedly, but she was just as clueless as they were to what the problem was. When the results of the testing came back, they were unsure of what they found because it was something so unusual, especially in children. I was diagnosed with an extremely rare brain disease called Central Nervous System Vasculitis. We were discombobulated and shocked because I was never a sickly child, I rarely ever even caught a cold! There are no know causes of this disease.

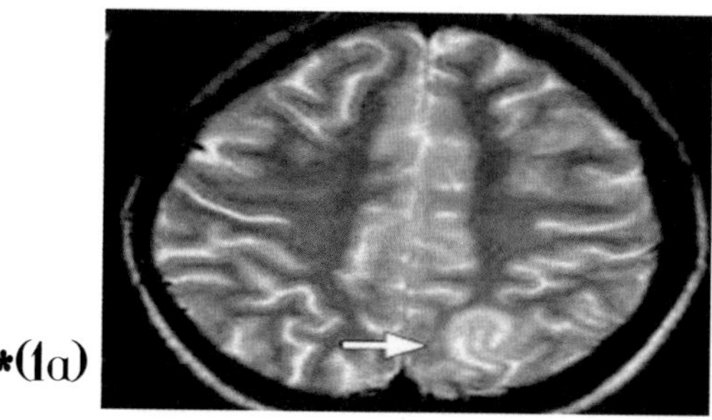
*(1a)

The doctors gave us two options, and considering my state of health, along with my young age, my mother was given the pressure to make the decision.

The two options given to her were to treat it with a plethora of strong medications or for me to have brain surgery. The downside of this disease being treated with medication alone would have been causing the inability for me to produce children. for me. My mother did not want to take that opportunity away from me, so the doctors needed to proceed with brain surgery. My mother said to the doctors, "I don't care, do whatever you have to do.Just save my baby!" My family and I received the news that I had to have a major procedure done. The doctor emphasized the gravity of the situation and told my parents that I may not live. I had 90% chance of death and 10% chance of living The procedure required the doctors to remove the inflammation that was on my brain. To say the least, the odds were not in my favor. My family was devastated to hear this but remained strong, nevertheless. When I went in for my first procedure, I needed to be given anesthesia. They rode me in on a gurney; on the way to the operation room, which was on a different floor than where my room was. My parents had on these white suits so they would be sterile, and I remember thinking they looked like the Michelin Man or marshmallows. This made me laugh despite the events that were about to happen. It makes me miss my childhood innocence.

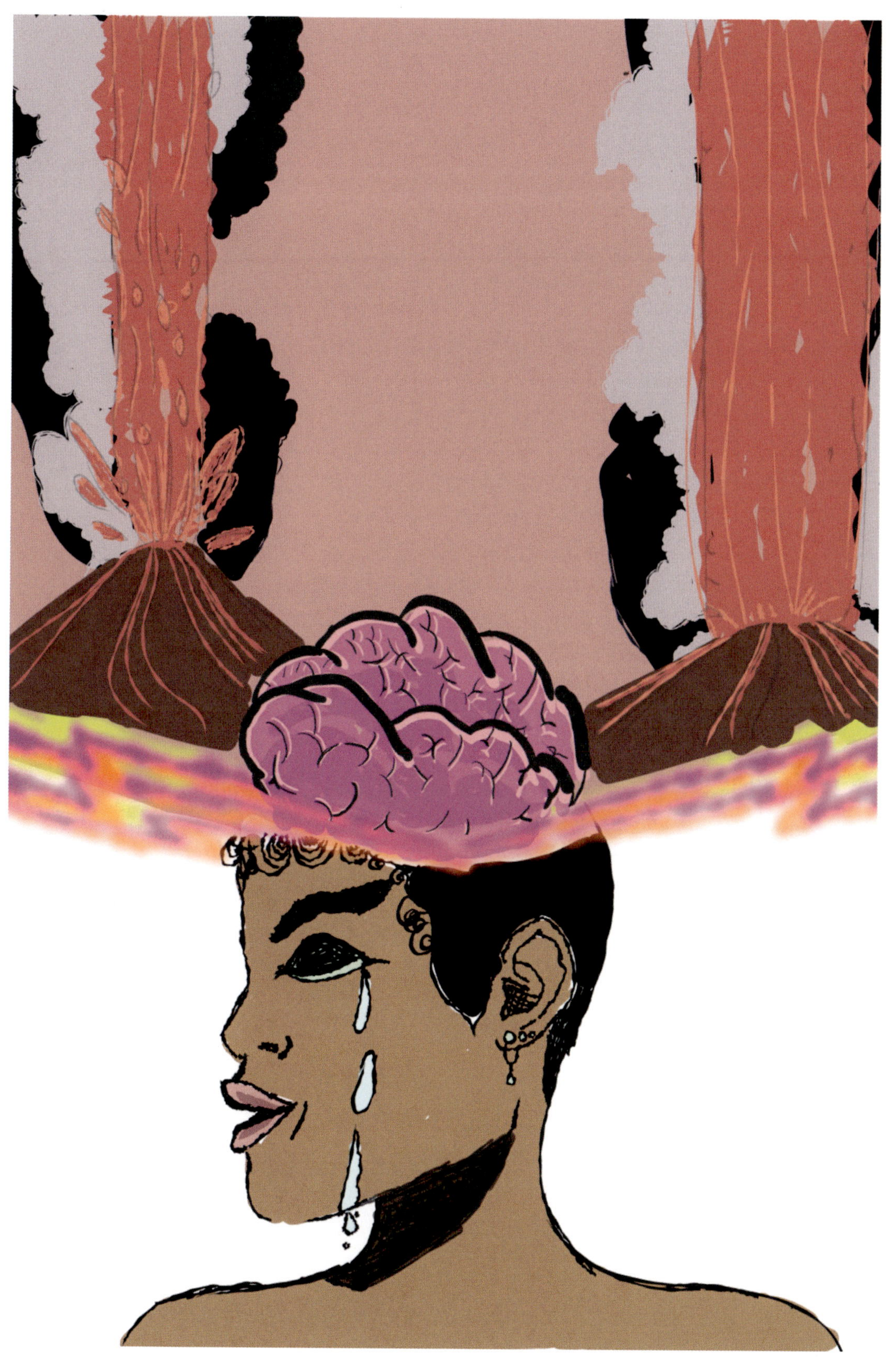

PTSD

When you look at me,
You see someone perfectly healthy
Little do you know,
Little ole me
Almost died at a time I was meant to be free.
But I was captured by disease
And tied down with feeding tubes, hospital gowns, and IV's
It's the seizure of a child you see,
Having a seizure as a child, ME
So when you look at me
You don't see all the PTSD it's caused me
Every time my head hurts, I think is back to get me
To take me back to its hospital headquarters
90% chance of death.
I will never forget those words.
Little do you know PTSD is not only for soldiers.
It's also for the ones who have to carry the weight of the world on their 2 shoulders!
Being the atlas of philosophy
In a world that doesn't provide us with any reciprocity!

So know when I switch up moods
You say I've gone insane
But what is crazy?
Different from the norm
So tell me, what is normal!?
Because even when I'm hormonal you call me crazy.
Well let's just hope this mental instability,
Doesn't cause any hostility between me,
And the Bourgeoisie

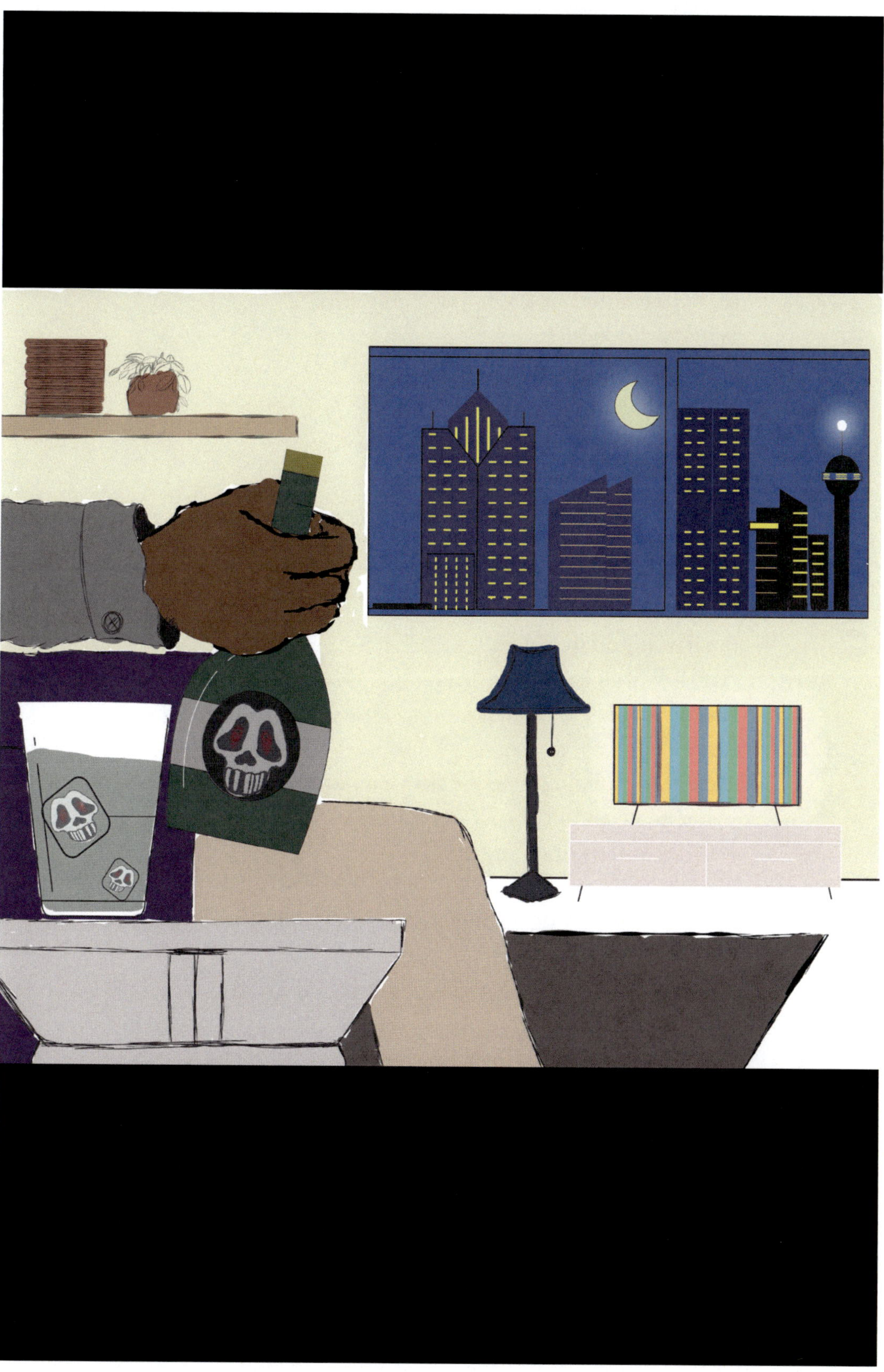

THE MONSTER

He doesn't even know it sneaks up on him...
Slowly, but surely, it gets to him.
He better watch out when it finds him,
When it finds him
It takes over his mind,
His soul,
It possesses him!
The monster has so much power
(but only when he gives it to him)
This monster,
is worse than the boogie man
Worse than any monster you can imagine. This is the devil in liquid form!
And it wants to make him a shot glass, So he can see his life shatter before his eyes. This is my message to him:
Just remember, whether they're swallowed or fired,
All shots can kill you!
It lures you in and captures you.

Making your thoughts askew, so you think it's ok to destroy everything around you!
Relationships with your daughters their mothers, and even your own.
Make you think it's not a big deal, right?
And it's brainwashing you.
Making you think this is good for you
So you can drown your sorrows in an ocean of toxicity.
So you let this devil kidnap you.
Zip Ties your hands,

Now you're emotionally and physically captive to his every demand!
I know You try to break free, but he is too strong!
Puts tape on your mouth
and now he's speaking for you.
Making every word more destructive than the last
He says, "Stop being a bitch ass nigga!"
Words like wildfire, that not even water can put out.
I see you can't scream for help.
Even though you know you need it.
So even when you break free from its captivity
All it takes is one stressful situation for the monster to come banging on your door, for more.
And you hear it say, iiiii'mmmm baaaacceckkkk.
The door creeks open.

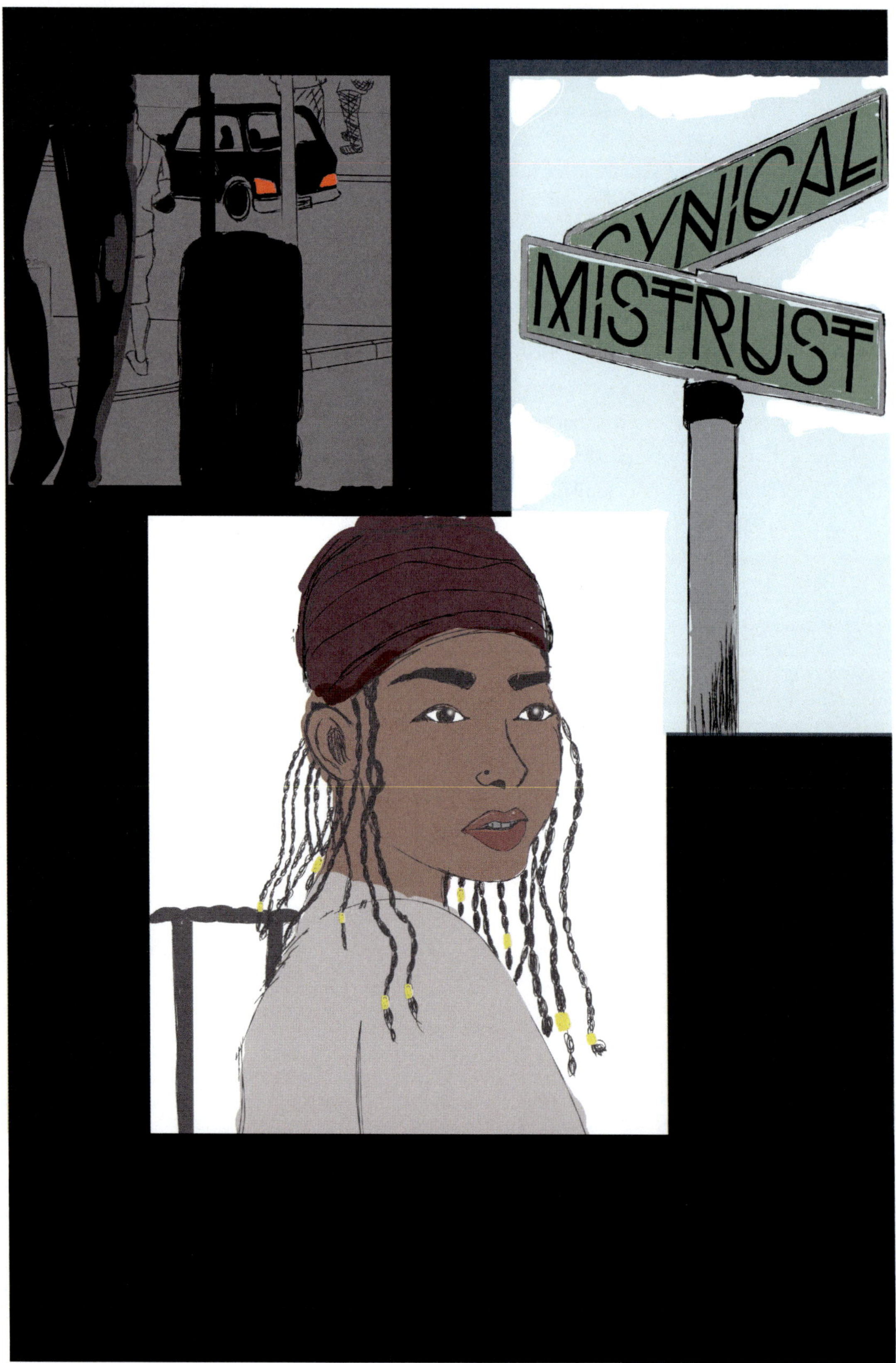
CYNICAL
MISTRUST

PLAYERS GAME

Answer me this,
Why do you put so much effort into screwing up my life?
Why do you think it's okay to retrieve the key to the locked door of my heart only to destroy me?
What do you gain?
The only thing I gain is the weight of the baggage I now have to carry around because of you!
Because of you,
I am standing at the corner of cynical and mistrust.
Waiting for my cab of loyalty That may never come.
I'm starting to see a cycle of you
Well, guys like you.
I just want to know,
What the fuck did they teach you in grade school!?
Let's be real, it sure as hell wasn't honesty!
Honestly… I'm done.

PART II

All writers get writer's block

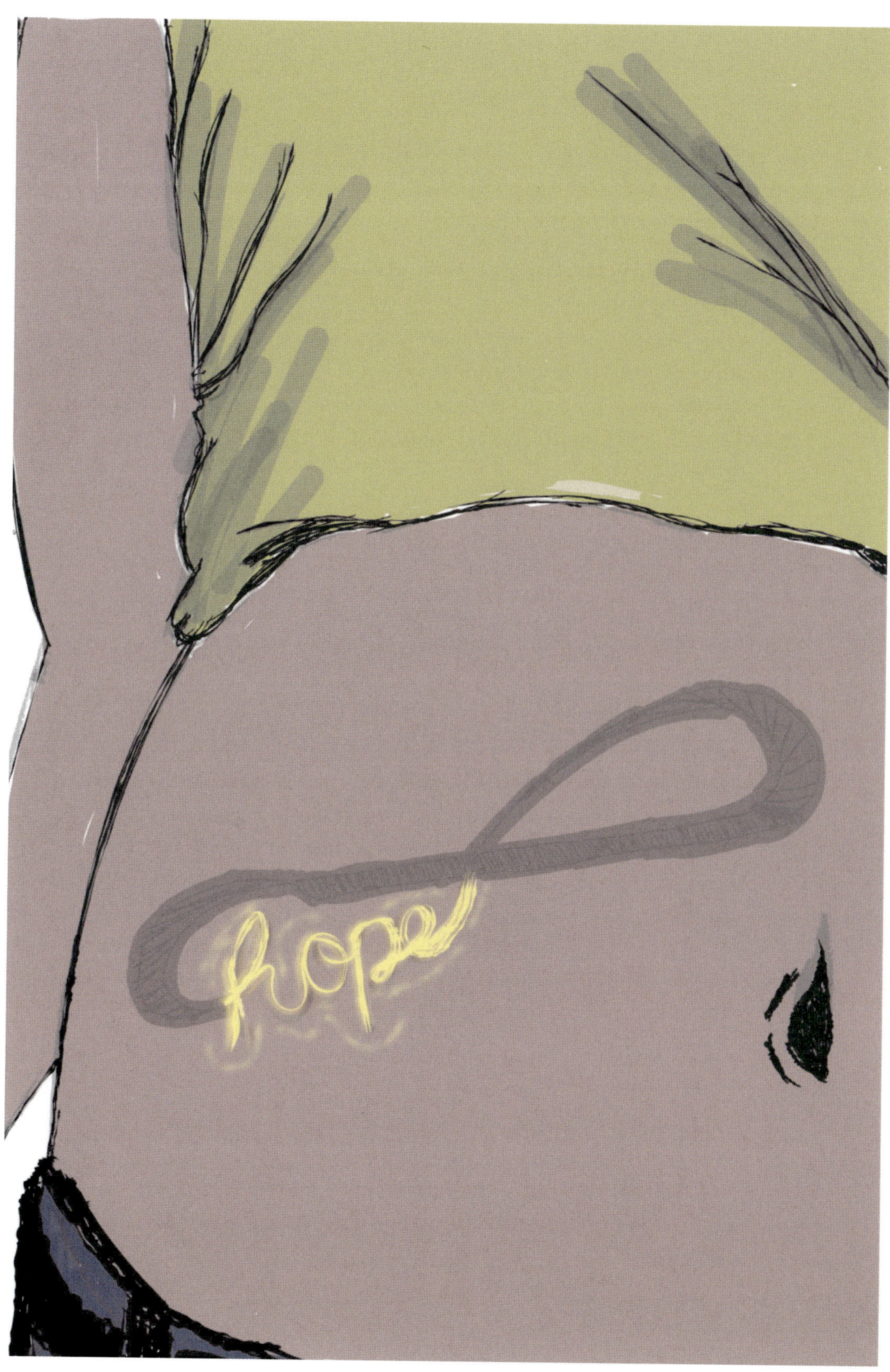
hope

ODE TO MY SCARS

I say ODE to the things that I "should" be ashamed of
but embrace.
I will NOT conform to social norms, So ode to my
scars for not hiding yourselves.
Thank you,
for being proud of who you are.
BEAUTIFUL,
Is what you are.
You are unashamed that you don't look like the rest
of my body.
And that's great.
Ode to my scars for reminding me of my own
strength
Whispering to me in times of doubt
"You can do this"
Then I remember, I'm a survivor!
Ode to my scars for telling your own story as you
project your voice loud and clear, to talk about our
journey.
Ode to my stretch marks! For showing me that I
needed to expand to take in all that was happening.
The Black Trojan Woman
Ode to my stretch marks. For reminding me that
yes, I was once overweight but that is not me now.
That makes me proud.
And yes I know that pride is a sin, But is it wrong to
be happy that I am
STILL HERE?
They make me who I am and remind me what I
stand for.

So forget scar removal.
My scars will **ALWAYS** be here, for me.

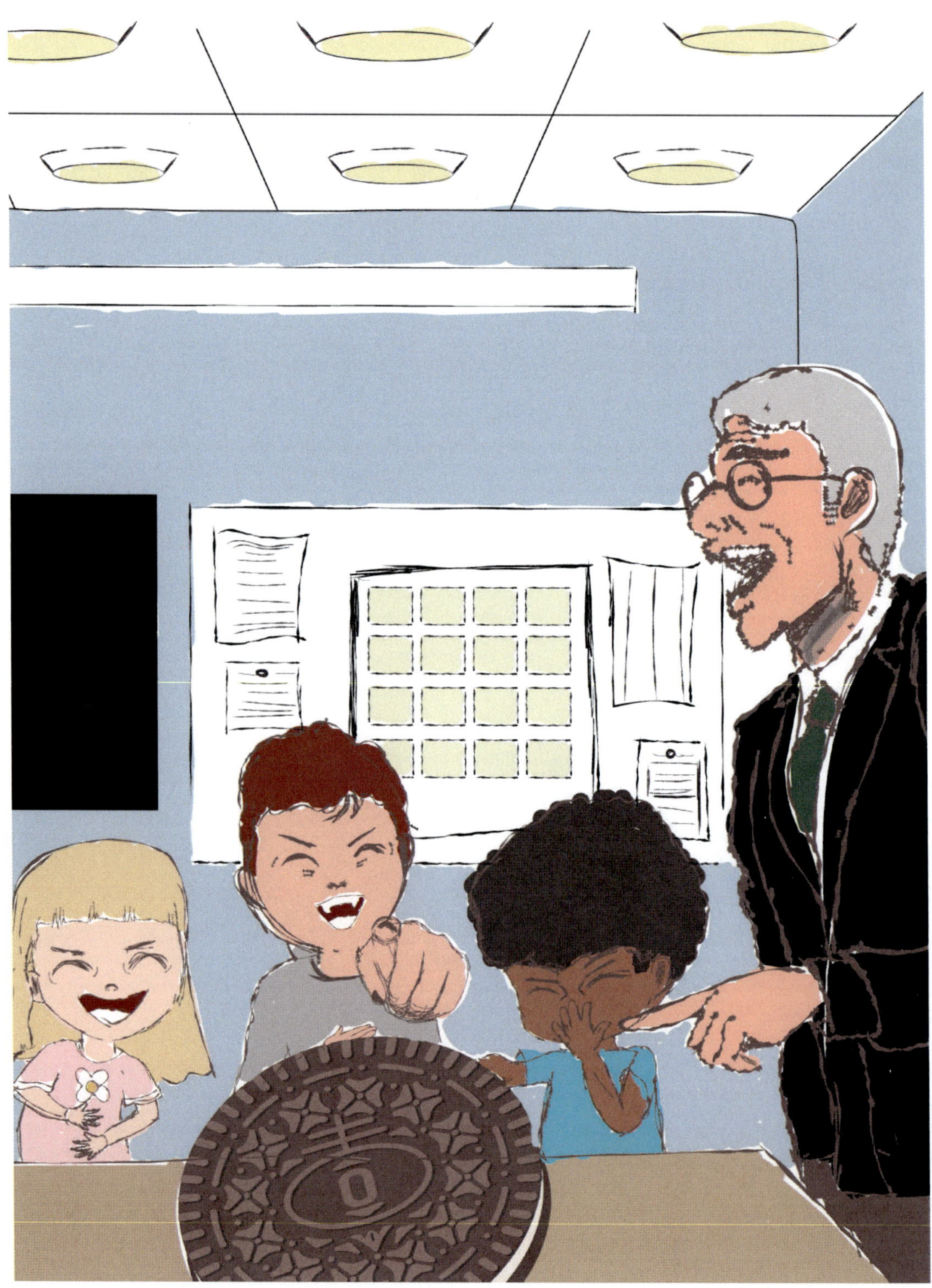

OREO

Oreo,
It's what they call me, You know, white on the inside,
black on the outside. They say this with a chuckle, as
to say I shouldn't be offended, as if it's not an insult
WELL, IT IS
It's like you're saying I'm a traitor to my own race.
So am I the Benedict Arnold of blacks?
They say "oh you're such a white girl" With that
mocking tone.
They say I "ACT WHITE"
But obviously not enough to be subject to white privi-
lege!
The caucasity to think your words can disrupt my
image
Is entitlement at its finest
When I see people eat Oreos they separate them,
Just how they separate people. You can't separate
any parts of me,
So I am not an Oreo.
I am...
Fierce, elegant strong, intelligent,
And so much more But I'm just me.

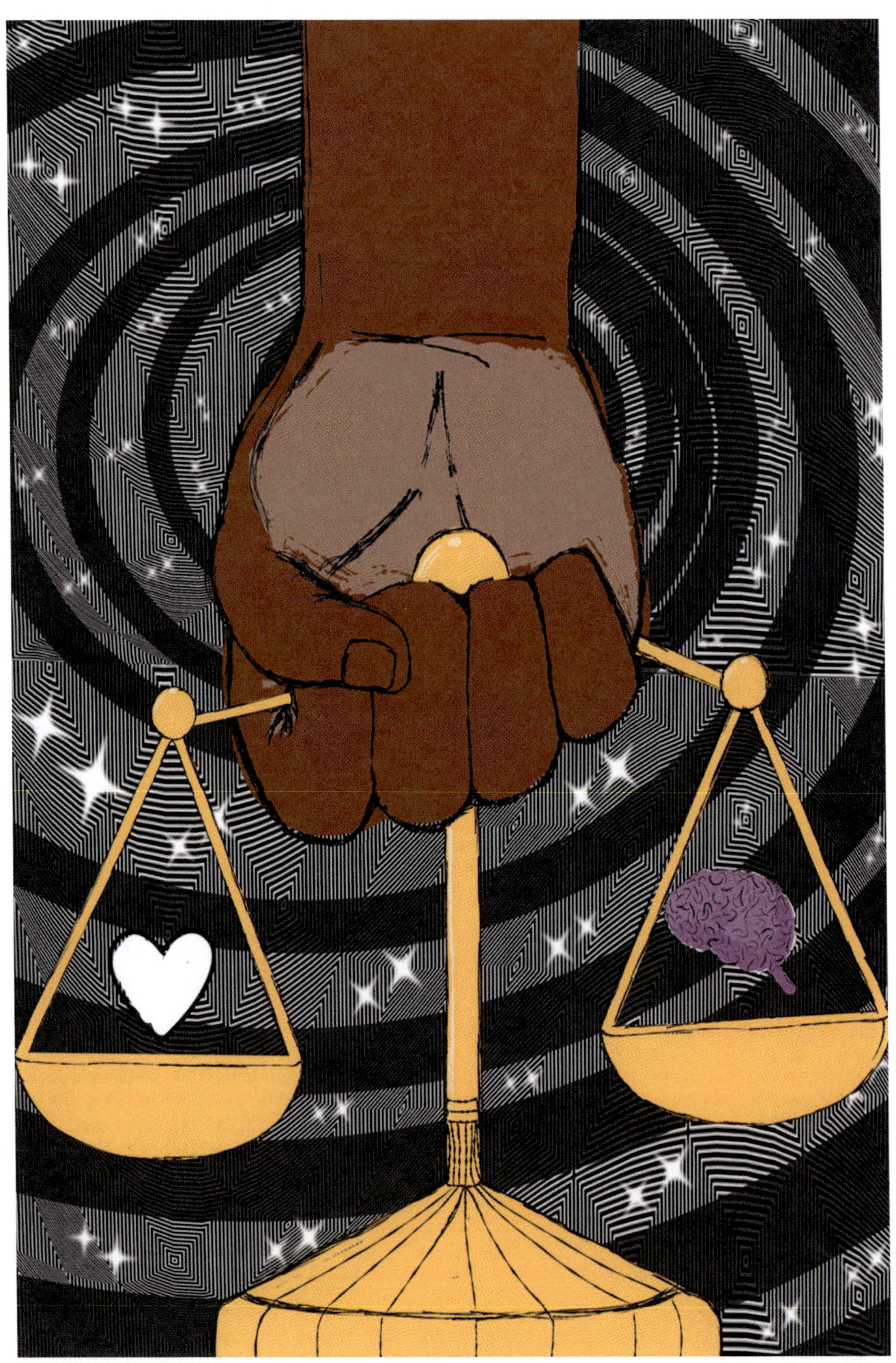

TYRANNY

My heart is swallowing the rest of my body, leaving me with no control.
I can't control myself when I'm with you.
That leaves me with the question of, Am I my heart or my mind?
If I am my mind, does that make me heartless If I am my heart, am I thoughtless? My heart is swallowing the rest of my body, Making it impossible to scream for help.
Yet, I am not sure that I want to.
What if I like this heart domination?
My heart is swallowing the rest of my body, and sometimes it feels swell.

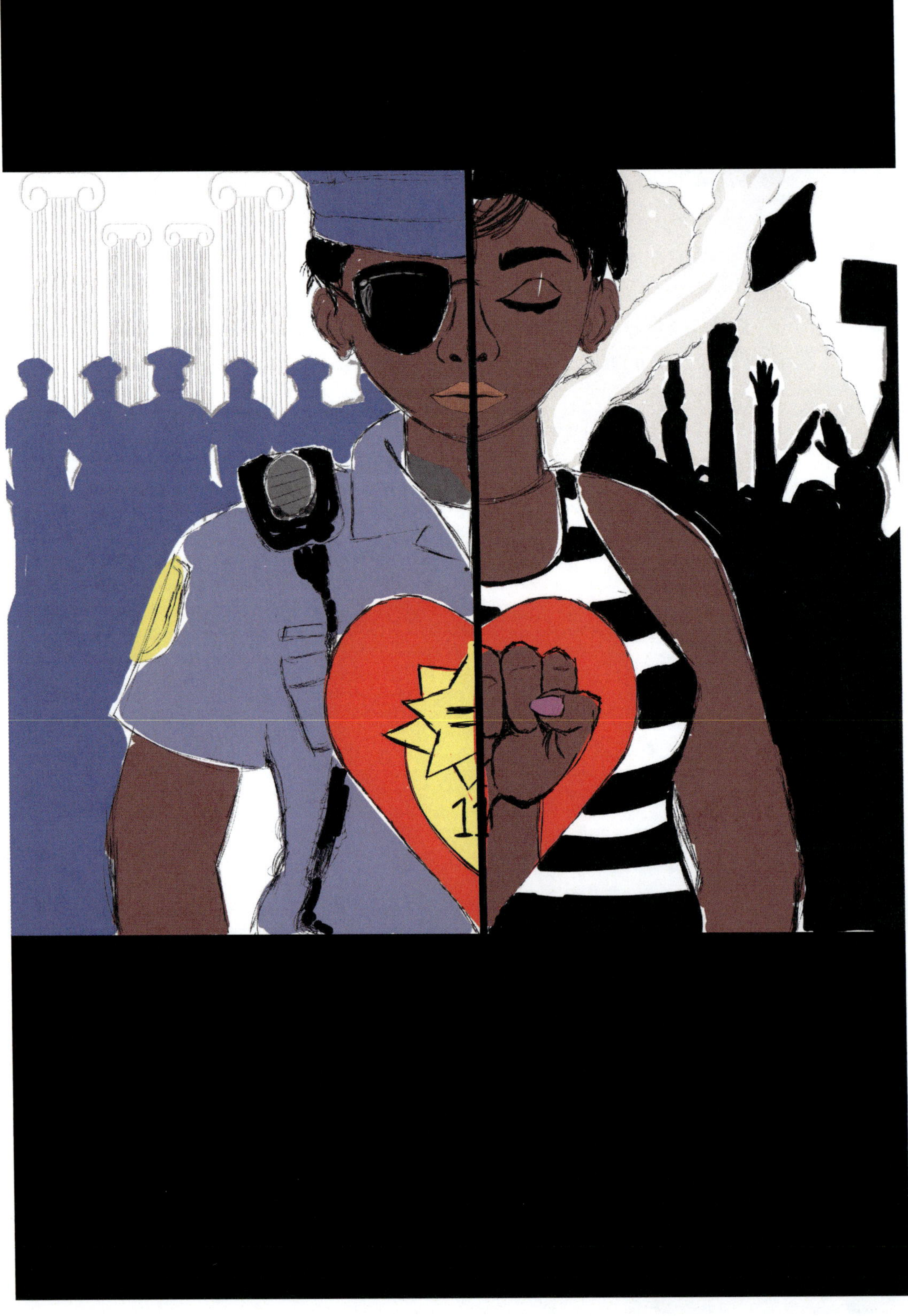

A LETTER FROM A BLACK COPS DAUGHTER

When you live in a black cop's home
You have this double consciousness,
Like how can I pay homage to Black Lives Matter,
When I still believe blue lives matter, Because her life matters!?
Cops taking our lives,
Yet she has given me life.
Living in this paradox
Is like being a circular box
How could you possibly be both? In this game of kill or be killed, and I can't imagine what it's like when it's your own people.
Face to face, with your own people. Now they go "oh that's two-faced" but you didn't stay in your place
When you decided to play with my mother's fate!
So how can I keep faith that she'll be safe?
When she's afraid to go into the bodega with her uniform on because civilians kill cops too.

You feel since a cop, that wasn't even her, harmed your family; you should kill her too?
The pain you were caused is now the pain I feel!
But thank God...
I hear the door open,
And she's home to make a meal.

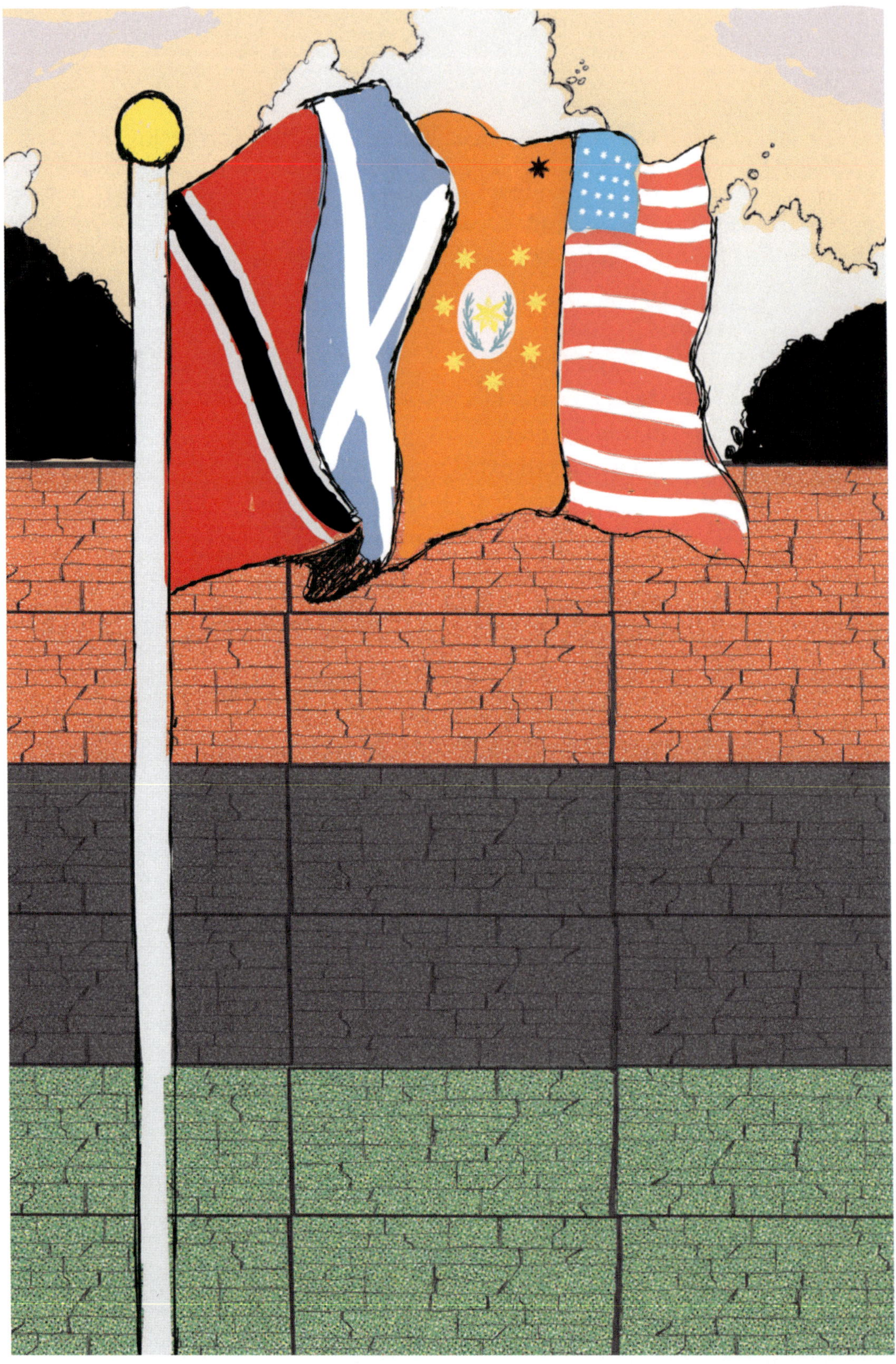

EMPTY CALORIES

I find myself questioning my identity.
Who am I?
I am not my mind or body
But this is all we understand.
I am a conglomerate of things
A sedimentary rock
I am Cherokee, i'se a Trini, American, even Scottish
But who's to say someone who looks like me can't be all of that.
You call me black because you don't know what else to call me You call me black, yet in reality, I'm brown.
You call me black because of the ruse of race rumored that it was real back in the 1500s.
Seems ignorance can be passed down through generations too.

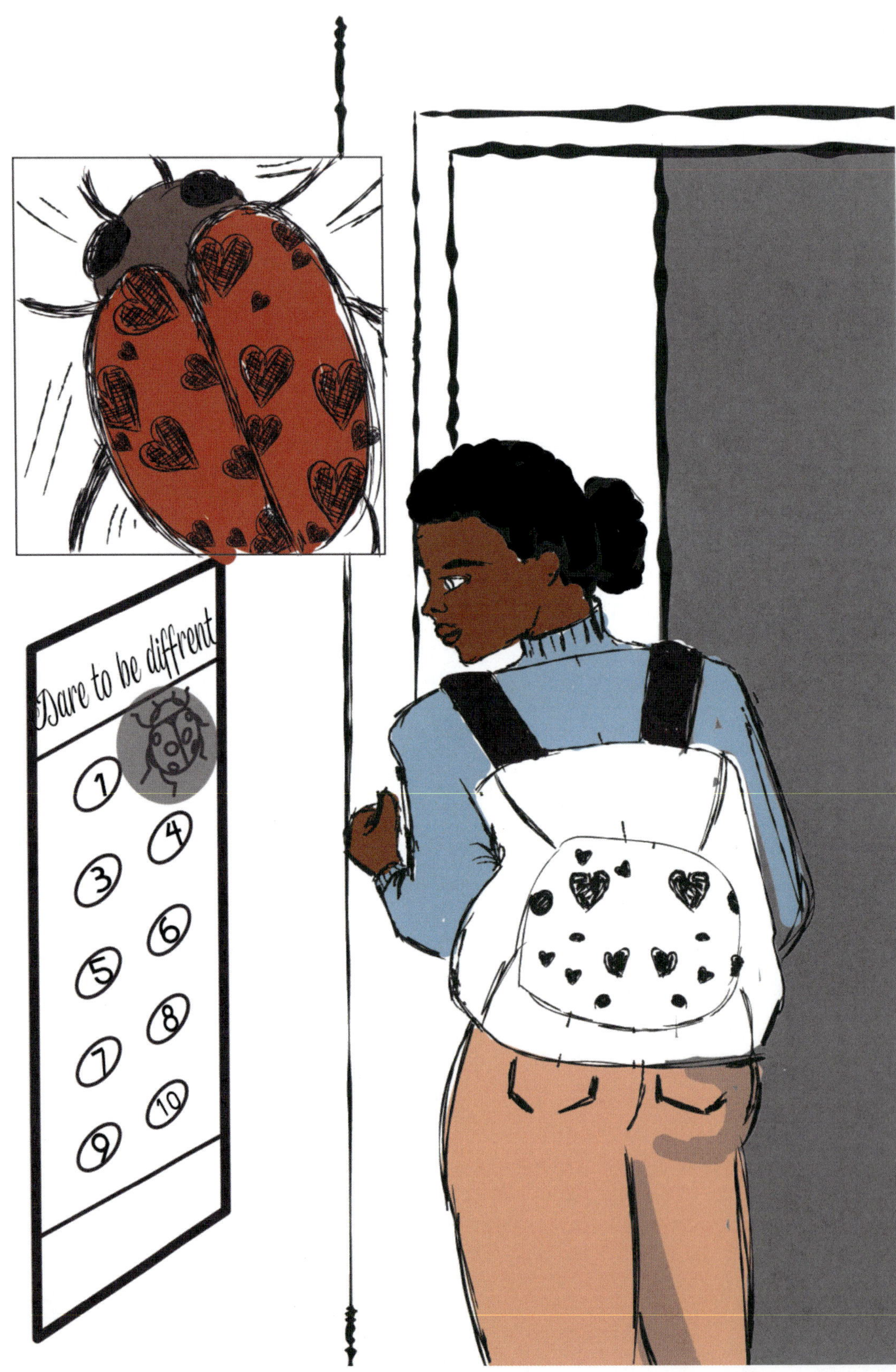
Dare to be diffrent
1
4
3
6
5
8
7
10
9

SWING

Sis doesn't know me from a can of paint.
But that doesn't matter when paint is white and
black,
Labeled with a ladybug
We are all ladybugs
As graceful, strong, and rare sight as a ladybug can
be. I remember the day I decided I wanted to be a
Sister With Interest Never Gone.
I saw a ladybug in the elevator.
That's how I knew Swing would take me to another
level.
Just as that elevator would.
A new level of womanhood
I said "I know I should,
This is a sign."
The thing about signs is they point you in the right
direction. > This one said right on white and black.
Despite all of the obstacles staring me down
I knew this was right for me And it always will be.

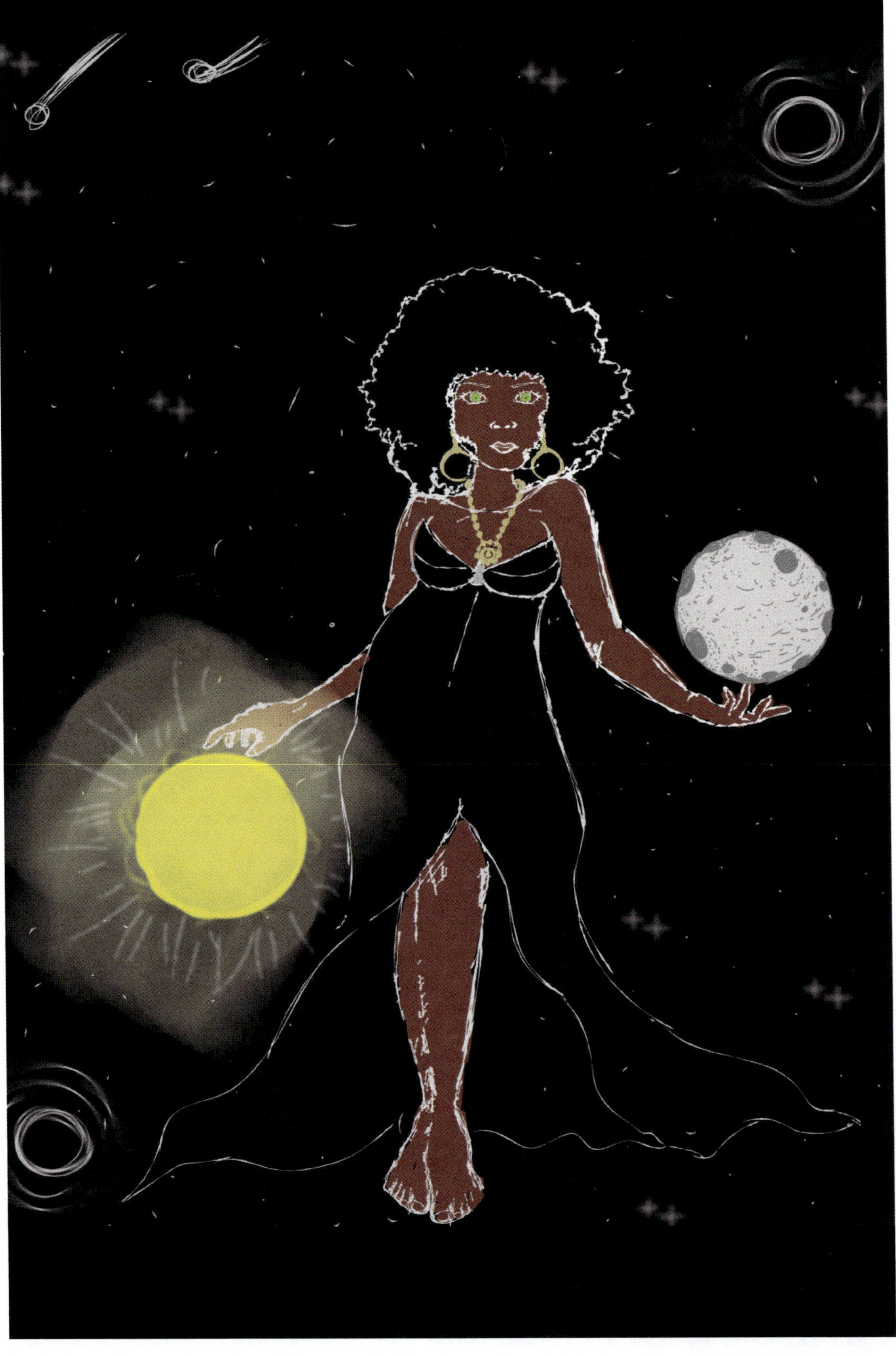

ENERGY

I've been through hell and back
So I use the energy from the flames I rose from to keep me going.
This is solar power.
I get my power from the sun
I guess that's y God made me a fire sign I get my beautiful brown hue from the sun, which looks like the same molasses that come from maple trees.
Though I don't use photosynthesis I am like a plant.
Growth is my goal
And I shall bear the fruits of my labor
I'm always happiest when it's sunny outside
I take every opportunity to absorb that vitamin D
So I can feel like me
Yanique, the goddess of beauty.

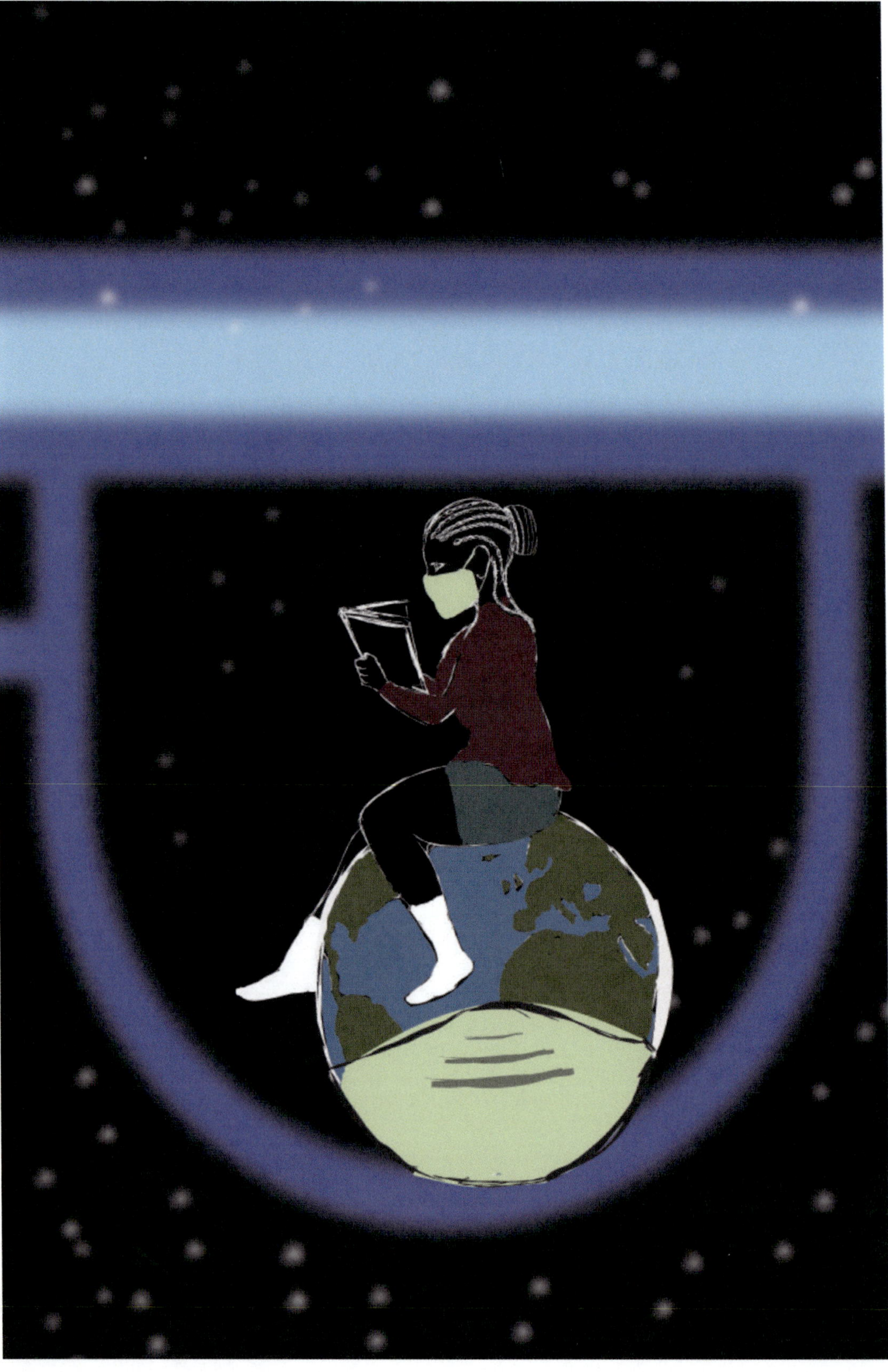

HINDSIGHT

After tragedy,
I often hear "what was the reason?"
I always thought that reason was me.
Self-blame is as destructive as the demolition of a building.
And that building was me,
Being torn down,
Floor by floor,
But then what is left?
He took all parts of me I thought were right with a single assaulting act of terror and trauma.
So I ask the question, was I the reason?
I used to be called fat by the skinny girls in my mostly white school.
Where the only other Black girl taunted me worse than the White girls!
I walked with a cane
Using it for support,
but what I really craved was the support of the friends I didn't have.
I used relaxers to control and maintain my mane.
But in Hindsight, nothing about me needed to be controlled or relaxed.
My magic was just a little too free for them
So they tried to fit me in a perm box that wasn't made for me.
Maybe that's why I'm only 5ft.
I could never grow.
So I sought out places that allowed for expansion
The misconception that therapy is only for people who are "crazy,"
is as toxic as drinking bleach to cure coronavirus.

It sounds just as ridiculous too.
Soul cleansing is hard work,
But it's priceless
Unfortunately, self-care comes with a price.
It is saying no to requests when you're over-
whelmed, it is learning to enjoy your own compa-
ny, it's learning how to be productive even when
you're feeling lazy.
I was always taught to treat others how I want to
be treated
but I never got taught the other side of the coin
Treat yourself how you want others to treat you.
After learning this,

Quarantine wasn't so bad,
It forced me to see my value to this world
Now I know loneliness is only a figment of the
imagination

Hindsight is 2020, and my vision is so clear
I have hopes and dreams for the new year

I hope that 2022 is good to me
I hope by this time next year I will be fluent in the
language of self-love
As fluent as my native tongue
English is my 1st
Self-love will be my 2nd
and this is the year for double blessings
This new vernacular will bring light into my
world!
I will learn every syllable, punctuation mark, silent
letter, and appropriate
pronunciation of every endearing and positive

word,
Of self-love!
I hope 2021 will let me leave it where it will be,
In the past.
I no longer want to carry the burden of the past on my back,
It feels like heavy textbooks filled with negativity.
All it does is weigh me down,
So I hope 2022 is good to me.
Because I'm trying to be good to me
And now I am.

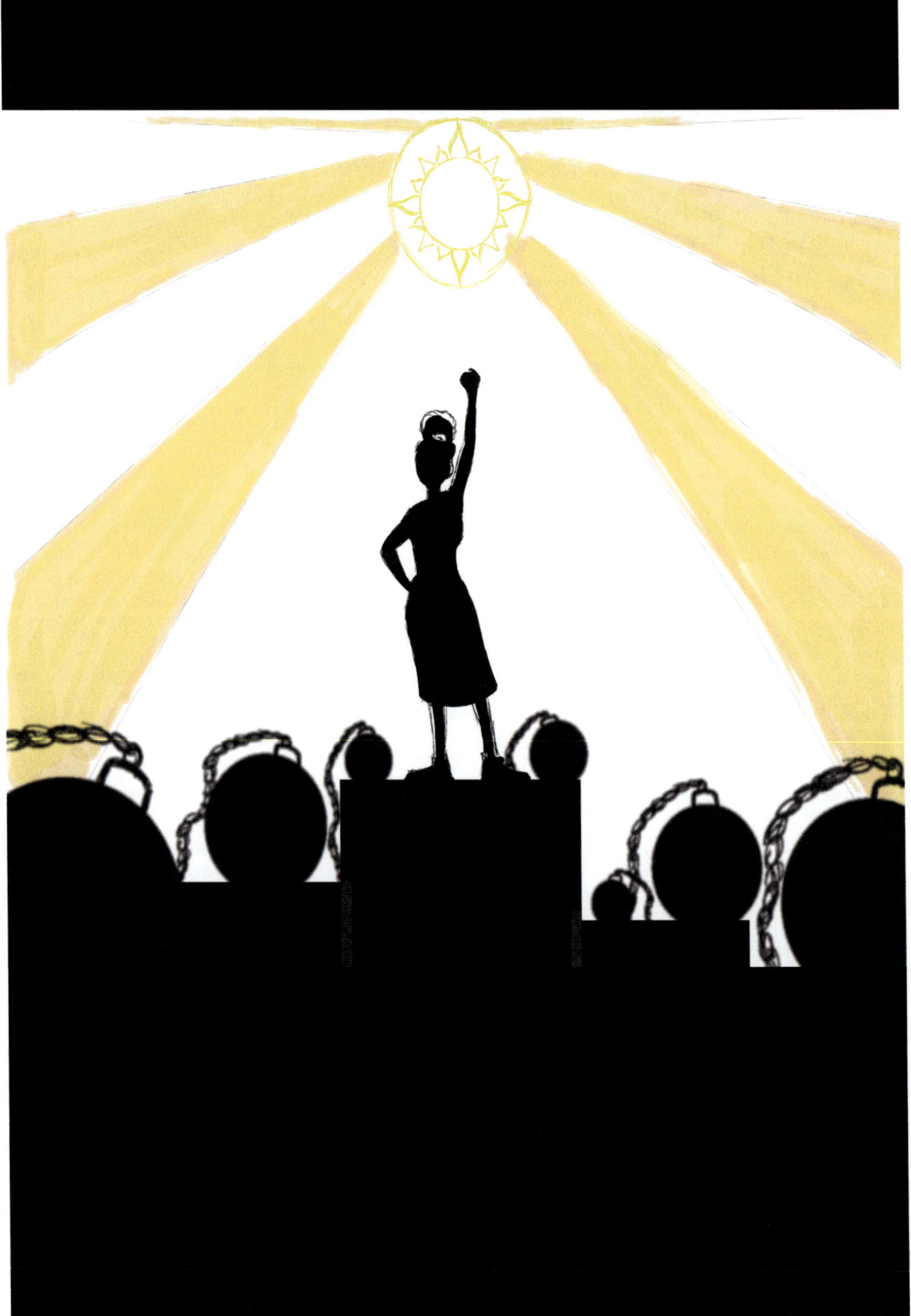

TRUE SELF LOVE

I've fallen in love with loving myself.
For the first time in a while, I feel whole.
Not to be confused with h o l e
So there's no room for discrepancy
There's no space for negativity Because I'm full.
Just as sure as I am that light drives out darkness
just as sure as I am about loving my darkness.
My Melanin rich skin,
My melanin-rich hair.
I've learned to get along with demons. We made a
contractual agreement
that they will stay quiet.
We all signed it too.
This is my Declaration of Independence
Signed Yanique Renwick, trauma, assault, bullying,
stepfather, death, disability, anxiety, fear.
Hereby agree to let Yanique be free!

REFERENCES

(1a) Brain Scan. (n.d.). https://www.vasculitis.org.uk/about-vasculitis/central-nervous-system-vasculitis. Retrieved from https://www.vasculitis.org.uk/about-vasculitis/central-nervous-system-vasculitis.

Made in the USA
Middletown, DE
01 April 2022